ALL
OUR
CATS

Anonymous: *Smutt*

ALL
OUR
CATS

KATOU FOURNIER
and
JACQUES LEHMANN

Translated from the French and revised by
WILLIAM A. PACKER

E. P. DUTTON   NEW YORK

This book is for
Ah-chu and Flossie
Ralph, Harriet, Henry, and Homer—
dear companions all

First published, 1985,
in the United States by E.P. Dutton, New York.

Originally published in France under the title *Chats Naïfs*.
Copyright © 1984 by Galerie Naïfs et Primitifs.
Translation copyright © 1985 by E. P. Dutton.
All rights reserved.

For information contact: E.P. Dutton,
2 Park Avenue, New York, N.Y. 10016

Library of Congress Catalog Card Number: 85-70805

Printed and bound by
Dai Nippon Printing Co., Ltd., Tokyo, Japan.
ISBN: 0-525-24357-7 (cloth)
0-525-48182-6 (DP)
Published simultaneously in Canada by
Fitzhenry & Whiteside Limited,
Toronto

COBE
10 9 8 7 6 5 4 3 2 1

First Edition

Contents

Foreword

The art of untutored artists, long considered a minor genre, is the result of popular imagery and workers' retirement. It was consecrated at the dawn of the century by the avant-garde artists who, by recognizing Henri Rousseau, the so-called Douanier, as a painter in his own right, thereby extended the borders of art to include naïve painting.

The last decades of the nineteenth century and the first decades of the twentieth bear the imprint of *l'Académie* in France. Adolphe William Bouguereau, Édouard Detaille, Jean Léon Gérôme, Jean Louis Ernest Meissonnier, and Pierre Puvis de Chavannes mark the high point of the Salon in painting. With extreme care these artists illustrate "grand subjects" (that genre called history painting) drawn from antiquity or the Bible, faithfully applying the lessons they were taught.

In order to avoid rivalry, these artists divided the painting subjects among themselves; one specialized in prehistory, another in Parisian salons and gatherings, yet another in Napoleonic campaigns.

A concern for realism, rather than personal creation, preoccupied them. Their chief concern was not the transmutation of appearances, but appearances themselves. Everything is measured, weighed, "starched," calculated, fixed, and deprived of emotion. Conversely, the naïve painter, unimpressed by overworked artifices, by contrived scenes of peasant life, of the rigid attitudes of passersby in the streets of soulless cities, paints what he sees and what he feels. He paints everyday life more with his

heart than with his head. It is this freshness, this utter sponta-
neity, that moves us so deeply. Propelled by what Kandinsky called
"the internal necessity," the untutored artist paints above all for
his own pleasure. He does not try to deliver a message, but tries
to convey his sense of wonder when confronted with the beauty
of nature or his memories of the scenes of his childhood. A
number of naïve painters take to art quite late in life, and at the
threshold of old age, they discover a world they had had no time
to appreciate earlier. All of a sudden, their main concern is to
re-create one by one the tiles of a roof, the leaves of a tree, or the
whiskers of a cat, often with the unconscious desire of giving
their subjects a degree of timelessness.

Yes, the purpose of the painting of these "singulars of art" is
to carry hope. The purity that it conveys is a diversion or recreation of the mind, a break in the monotony of daily routine. It
teaches us to watch closely a world that the naïve painter has
re-created according to his own heart.

Yet although only recently recognized, naïve painting was
not born, as is usually thought, with the works of the Douanier
Rousseau. Actually, when one tries to trace it back in time, one
notices that it has always been an integral part of the history of
man. In the very stone of Lascaux and Rouffignac, our distant
ancestors etched bison, deer, and mammoths to appeal for favor
for the hunts to come.

A projection of the artist's desire, this spontaneous form of
painting is in some ways similar to today's naïve art. At about
the time these rupestrian paintings were discovered, the artistic
value of folk creations was being recognized. On the margin of
official art there had developed a form of art engendered by the
needs of daily life and rooted in the instincts of the people. The
tools that had been invented by the village craftsman in order to
plow the earth and carry water from the well were often carved
with such fondness as to become real works of art.

Similarly, painted shop signs, often made with poetical realism, call the attention of passersby to the cobbler's or the
cooper's shop.

Other significant folk-art objects are the religious ex-
votos, asking for God's mercy or thanking Him for His
goodness. These ex-votos, brightly colored and movingly
designed, decorate the walls of numerous chapels.

In nineteenth-century America, craftsmen traveled from coast
to coast, from small towns to hamlets, announcing their coming
in advance, seeking commissions for portraits they would exe-

Anonymous: *Dressed in a Ruff*

cute on the spot. With varying success, these limners applied their talent to reproducing what they saw. Because they had not learned how to paint, they have been lumped together with the naïve artists, although their obstinacy in tackling only reality sets them apart from the latter. The naïve painter grants much freedom to his imagination. As Anatole Jakovsky so justly put it: "Naïve painting is above all an *état d'âme* [a condition of the soul]. It is a mirror that reflects nothing and visualizes still less. It is turned toward what is hidden, toward those dreams and private ghosts that magic—much more skillfully than colors or brushes—knows how to conjure up."

From a chronological point of view, naïve painting cannot be incorporated into the history of art; it has always run parallel to it. Indifferent to the various tendencies that feed it, serenely scanning the world, naïve painting is oblivious to external modes or fashions.

The element of irrationality that goes into naïve painting is the warrant of its timelessness. "I am not the one who paints, it is something else at the tips of my fingers that does," stated Rousseau.

Nowadays, naïve painting still runs along a path of its own. But in the latter half of the twentieth century, the way of looking at it has changed somewhat. In effect, some young painters have chosen it from the beginning as their exclusive means of expression. They rejected the inherited culture in order to be able to revisit the world with new eyes.

Besides, even if Rousseau and André Bauchant took to their brushes only after the age of forty, we forget too easily that Louis Vivin started painting at the age of nineteen and Camille Bombois at the age of twenty-four. The works of the new generation have, according to Jakovsky, "that aspect that is slightly bedazzled, ingenuous, peaceful, heralded and happy, in short a festive aspect that characterizes without exception all their paintings."

Impervious, it would seem, to the alienation of modern life, the naïve painters have recaptured the joy and freshness of life. Not seeking to become professionals in painting, they would rather let their brushes run freely on the canvas, invoking their dreams. They take us along into the colorful memories of their travels in wonderland or walk with us along the streets of big cities, discovering there a latent beauty.

The cat, a privileged subject as this book testifies, is the friend

Ammi Phillips: *Young Girl with Her Pets*

of the naïve artist. Because the cat represents at once the synthesis between commonplace daily life and mystery, the ordinary and the supernatural, it is very often a source of inspiration to the naïve painter.

Several years ago, the Museum of American Folk Art in New York City devoted a large exhibition to the cat in naïve painting. Anonymous canvases of the nineteenth century, together with fascinating paintings created by Morris Hirshfield in the twentieth century, depicted all sorts of cats: black cats, white cats, alley cats, pedigreed cats, sleeping cats, sitting cats, mouse-hunting cats, lonely cats, sociable cats, cats with a child, mysterious or friendly cats...

The subject of this beautiful book is the cat in naïve paintings by artists from Europe and America. Let us immerse ourselves in this fascinating wonderland and bet, why not, that by the time we have turned the last page our vision of things will be somewhat different and that we, like the great Stendhal, will be convinced that naïveté is the sublimity of ordinary life.

Robert Bishop
Director,
Museum of American Folk Art,
New York

Of Cats
and
Men

The cat has been sharing man's life for the past five thousand years, half as long as his rival, the dog.

For five thousand years he has been curling up, round as a ball, on people's laps, burying his little nose in the comforting warmth of his underbelly.

For five thousand years he has been staking out some soft mattress for his favorite resting place, more accommodating than the hard straw mat assigned him by the ancient Egyptians.

It was those Egyptians, in fact, who first domesticated a feline breed—the Kaffir race, ancestor of the *Felis domestica*, with short hair marked by fine horizontal stripes on the tail and paws, and sometimes on the torso, too.

More than merely a pet, he soon became man's aide and protector, defending his crops against rats, his silkworms and papyrus against every kind of marauding rodent. Thus, he helped to stave off famine, ensure the textile trade against bankruptcy, and salvage ancient culture from oblivion.

Content with apartment life in the twentieth century, the cat makes no objections to his restricted living space, where he can spend most of the daylight hours snoozing; indeed, he spends two thirds of his entire life in slumber.

And how does he spend the remaining one third?

Feeding, hunting, attending to his toilette, playing, and, if given the chance, loving.

If a master, late for the office, forgets to serve his cat's morning meal, the oversight poses no problem. The hungry cat will find his way to a cache of victuals, generally stored away in the cabinet under the kitchen sink.

Should some intrepid mouse dare to risk his life and huddle close to a convenient hole in the wall—an escape hatch recommended in case of an emergency—to watch his deadly foe at work, he will behold an amazing spectacle. The cat rises up on his hindquarters, leans his forepaws against the cabinet, turns the knob with one paw, opens it, and creeps inside. There he surveys all the possibilities from which to make his choice— today, it will be a cookie. He tears open the top of the cookie box with his teeth, pulls out his breakfast with one paw, and nibbles.

At no stage does he encounter any obstacles. Indeed, this exploit demands nothing like the patience and ingenuity required to stalk a pigeon in the park across the street. In this case, the cat sits at the picture window in the living room under the illusion that he is out of doors, and prepares to bag his prey; but the glass panes thwart him. Since he is no Alice passing through the looking glass, he can only contemplate in his mind's eye what a clever hunting cat would do if he could: curl up at the foot of a plane tree feigning innocence, wait for some dear old lady to scatter a week's accumulation of bread crumbs over the grass, and wait, motionless, for a swarm of pigeons to swoop down on them. Without stirring a muscle, he lets them peck away, unaware, while he marks out the most likely victim. He measures the distance he must jump to land squarely on the unsuspecting bird and takes a flying leap.

This is standard procedure for the smart hunter-cat, but what he does with his catch once he has nabbed it depends on his character. In general, he will fall into one of three categories:

1. Unsentimental by nature, he will lose no time in doing his pigeon in and eating it up.

2. A mischievous joker, he will release the bird, tease it, and pounce on it again several times before consigning it to its doom.

3. Like Type 2, he harasses his bird, but so clumsily that it escapes his clutches and flutters off to the safety of the sky, leaving the cat to console himself with what remains of the bread crumbs—which the other pigeons have wisely abandoned—if such humble fare agrees with him.

Unappeased, the apartment cat soon forgets his misfortune and turns his attention to other activities—chasing his tail or

Zofia Szalowska: *The Trio*

imagining some exotic adventure, like a safari in Africa. Unaccountably, this incites him to scamper from room to room, occasionally interrupting the race to explore inside the bathtub or crawl under a bed in pursuit of imaginary wildlife.

Worn out at length by these exertions, he retires to his corner and begins to groom himself. He licks a paw until it is moist enough to scrub those areas he cannot reach with his tongue, such as the ears inside and out, the eyelids, and the areas between eyes and ears.

All felines are endowed with prodigious intelligence; nothing in their actions, however surprising, is by any means extraordinary. Motivated by identical instincts, each will react in the same way to any given situation.

Such as answering the call of the female siren who lives next door. Pricking up his ears, the tomcat will promptly abandon the comforts of home and vanish into the night.

But her vocalizing has also aroused all the other toms in the neighborhood.

Lying on the grass in the darkness, she emits her incantations. A horde of pretenders gathers from all directions and surrounds her. The mass courtship begins. It will last for hours, while she takes her own good time to look her suitors over and decide which one would be the best choice. Thus, the lucky winner must bide his time to savor the fruits of his victory, even though the culminating act will be consummated with lightning speed.

Instances of sexual fidelity between males and females are not frequent in the cat world, but neither are they altogether rare.

Like many members of the human race, felines sometimes nurture odd tastes in their erotic preferences. Snow White, for example, the patrician Persian hosted by designer Jean-Michel Folon, will copulate only with an oversized, yellow tom that roams her rural district, even though his social status is far beneath hers. But, as some people say, "the heart has its reasons."

Mating over, the she-cat forsakes her role as community trollop for that of pregnant mother soon to give birth. For the multiple blessed event, an appropriate place has been put at her disposal in the cellar, but she prefers the half-open drawer of the Hepplewhite chest in the guest room, where she can purr to her heart's content.

Lying on one side, her eyes half closed, and breathing in short gasps, she seems to be fully in control of every internal development. As the hours pass, her purring grows louder. Suddenly she rears up, flops back, rises again, and finally settles down quietly

Zofia Szalowska: *George Brassens with His Cat*

to produce a brace of kittens. Delighted with her little brood, she willingly allows them to monopolize her completely. With adoration she grooms her offspring, nuzzles them with her nose, and encourages them to suckle. Nothing can distract her, not even the plaintive pleas of their father, or her mistress's insistent blandishments. During the postnatal period, she will spurn all importunate males and refuse to play the role of a house cat; for the time being, she is a full-time mother and nobody's pet.

In *Through the Looking Glass,* Lewis Carroll described a mother-cat tending her kittens:

> The way Dinah washed her children's faces was this: first she held the poor thing down by its ear with one paw, and then with the other paw she rubbed its face all over, the wrong way, beginning at the nose: and just now, as I said, she was hard at work on the white kitten, which was lying quite still and trying to purr—no doubt feeling that it was all meant for its good.

During the first weeks of their sojourn on earth, the irresistible little creatures establish their independence. By some infallible instinct, each one chooses a nipple and claims it for its own throughout most of the lactation period. With the tip of its tiny snout, the kitten sniffs out its reserved milk supply whenever it feels hungry. During her brood's first days, the mother almost never abandons them, taking time out only long enough to feed herself.

At the end of four or five weeks she begins to wean them with overflowing love and exemplary patience. Meowing a summons to the dinner plate, she prods them to acquire a taste for rice and scraps of meat, which they do with such alacrity that they will catch on after only a few servings. Most often she will not feed herself until they have eaten their fill.

Now comes the time for recreation. For the very young kitten it soon takes the form of intense curiosity about the world around him, and he sets out to explore its secrets. Attempting to evade his mother's strict surveillance, he repeatedly ventures beyond the designated limits of his living space. His inquisitive instinct is matched only by his temerity.

He sniffs the floor, crouches behind the crossbars of a chair, helps make beds, sometimes slipping under the covers to see what's there, chases a skein of yarn across the rug, unraveling it

Marta Gaspar: *Perched in a Sea of Pastel*

into a hopeless tangle, and trips over himself as he goes in pursuit of a fly. His little legs are still too unstable to catch it.

Weary at last of these solitary amusements, he climbs up on his master's lap and puts a paw on the page of the book he is reading to engage his attention and urge him to join in the fun. Touched, the man lays his book aside, however engrossing it may be, and begins to play with him. If he is understanding, he will heed his kitten's pleas and thereby help him to grow up into a normal, well-adjusted cat. The rapport a master establishes in play with his kitten will determine its personality in adulthood.

No less than an infant child, *Felis domestica* will bear the scars or benefits of his early conditioning all through life. A kitten rejected in play may well show symptoms of mental disorder in the future (good morning, Herr Freud!); whereas in play he will learn something about himself and the world—how to familiarize himself with his environment and come to terms with mankind.

Happy master, happy cat. Indifferent master, reclusive cat.

More than anyone, Colette knew how to conduct meaningful conversations with her feline pets. The only risk you run in befriending a cat, she once said, is the risk of enriching yourself.

Cats figured so prominently in her life that she often portrayed them in her books. In "The Cat," one of her best-known short stories, Alain finds himself torn between his adored cat and his fiancée Camille. His two mistresses are locked in a bitter feud; Camille plots to kill Saha, but the cat outwits her and emerges the victor.

The bond uniting Alain and Saha is no less passionate than a love match between a man and a woman. In Alain, Saha evokes a passion as intense as any he could feel for a woman, thus, not surprisingly, provoking Camille's jealousy.

The man-cat rapport is depicted as much through verbal communication as through sensual, physical complicity.

A flash of silver shot out and scuttled against Alain's leg like a fish.

"Ah, there you are, Saha. I've been looking for you. Why didn't you come to the table this evening?"

"Merroin," the cat replied.

"What, merroin? Why merroin? Is that any way to talk?"

"Merroin," the cat insisted. "Merroin."

Tenderly, he stroked her back, softer than rabbit fur, his

Evelyne Blot: *Playfulness*
Saint-Côme: *Engulfed in Daisies*

Gisèle Pierlot: *Slumbering with Cats*

Magdalena Shummer: *Girl with Three Cats*

Setsuko Uno: *My Little Black Cat*

fingers ending at the small, damp nostrils, dilated by her vigorous purring.

"That's my cat . . . my cat," he murmured.

"Merroin," Saha confirmed in a low tone, "merroin."

. . . .

From a distance, Saha eyed him gravely in the depths of the mirror.

"I'm coming," she indicated.

He threw himself down on the fresh sheets and arranged her on the bed in position to begin their ritual love play. . . .

"My lovely, lovely little puss with the fat cheeks. You're my sapphire dove, my pearl-tinted siren."

He turned out the light. The cat stepped daintily on his chest, and penetrated under his silk pajamas with a paw, touching the skin so lightly that the gesture stirred a disquieting pleasure in him.

Seven more days and seven more nights, and then a new life under another roof with an amorous young woman he had not yet conquered. Again and again he drew his hand over the cat's soft, warm fur, exuding a scent like pine bark or newly sawn wood or fresh grass. Purring heavily in the darkness, she kissed him, with the moist tip of her snout grazing Alain's lips—a momentary cat's kiss she rarely conceded.

"Ah, Saha! Our nights . . ."

(translated by Morris Bentinck)

By nature deeply affectionate, the cat seeks endearments and caresses. More than any other animal, he needs physical contact and never ceases to look for it. Sometimes he will rub his little head against a friendly cheek, sometimes his frame against the house dog's coarse hair. He demands fondling; it reminds him of his earliest moments in life when he reveled in his mother's warmth, her reassuring tongue licks, her tender gestures and unfailing presence.

Leaving these nostalgic reveries behind, the cat takes comfort in grooming himself. Whenever he feels doubts or fears of any kind, he will assuage them with a washing.

Nothing pleases him more than the felicitous gibberish uttered by a young boy, as he is cradled in the child's arms. By some unfathomable phenomenon, the cat understands every

Arlette Laville: *Amelia and Her Cat*

Zofia Szalowska: *Eleanor*

word, even if no one else does. He responds by modulating his purrs to the rhythm of his pleasure.

In his popular short story "The Cat That Walked by Himself," Rudyard Kipling imagined a cat making himself indispensable to an infant boy by becoming his protector; thus, he is the first of his species to secure a position in human society, which has hitherto rejected him for lack of proper qualifications.

One evening Bat said, "There is a Baby in the Cave. He is new and pink and fat and small, and the Woman is very fond of him."

"Ah," said the Cat, listening, "but what is the Baby fond of?"

"He is fond of things that are soft and tickle," said the Bat. "He is fond of warm things to hold in his arms when he goes to sleep. He is fond of being played with. He is fond of all those things."

"Ah," said the Cat, listening, "then my time has come."

Next night Cat walked through the Wet Wild Woods and hid very near the Cave until morning-time, and Man and Dog and Horse went hunting. The Woman was busy cooking that morning, and the Baby cried and interrupted. So she carried him outside the Cave and gave him a handful of pebbles to play with. But the Baby still cried.

Then the Cat put out his paddy paw and patted the Baby on the cheek, and it cooed; and the Cat rubbed against its fat knees and tickled it under its fat chin with his tail. And the Baby laughed and the Woman heard him and smiled. . . .

"A blessing on that Wild Thing whoever he may be," said the Woman, straightening her back, "for I was a busy woman this morning and he has done me a service."

For rendering her this service, the Cat was granted the right to come and go as he liked in the Cave. But he wanted more, therefore he was obliged to complete his conquest.

But the Baby cried because the Cat had gone away, and the Woman could not hush it, for it struggled and kicked and grew black in the face.

"O my Enemy and Wife of my Enemy and Mother of my Enemy," said the Cat, "take a strand of the wire that you are spinning and tie it to your spinning-whorl and drag it

Fanny Darnat: *Andrew*

Mimi Vang Olsen: *Cat and Kittens*

Cellia Saubry: *The Couple*

Marie-Hélène Véran: *Family Portrait*

Susan Tantlinger: *Patience*

Fanny Darnat: *Under the Table*

Sophie Sirot: *My Neighbor's Cat*

Monique Valdeneige: *Togetherness in a Basket*

Christine Cipriano: *Girl in Blue Posing with Her Friends*

Monique Valdeneige: *The Trollop*

Monique Valdeneige: *Having Lunch*

Zofia Szalowska: *Astonishment*

Marta Gaspar: *Cat and Pearls*

Brigitte Mailliet: *Moon and Her Child*

Susan Tantlinger: *The Little One*

Anne Gavarni: *The Cats Are in the Garden*

Christine Cipriano: *The Siamese Family on a Flowered Settee*

Didier Richard: *On the Threshold*

along the floor, and I will show you a magic that shall make your Baby laugh as loudly as he is now crying."

"I will do so," said the Woman, "because I am at my wits' end; but I will not thank you for it."

She tied the thread to the little clay spindle and drew it across the floor, and the Cat ran after it and patted it with his paws and rolled head over heels, and tossed it backward over his shoulder and chased it between his hind-legs and pretended to lose it, and pounced down upon it again, till the Baby laughed as loudly as it had been crying, and scrambled after the Cat and frolicked all over the Cave till it grew tired and settled down to sleep with the Cat in its arms.

"Now," said the Cat, "I will sing the Baby a song that shall keep him asleep for an hour." And he began to purr, loud and low, low and loud, till the Baby fell fast asleep. The Woman smiled as she looked down upon the two of them and said, "That was wonderfully done. No question but you are very clever, O Cat."

The cat understands man and man tries to understand the cat, but he eludes us. Within him is a dark area no human will ever penetrate. Yet here lies the wellspring of the complexity and strength that define the relationship between cat and man. The cat offers only what he is willing to give, firmly maintaining the mystery of his true nature, as if to defend a secret realm to which he alone has access. This is his freedom.

Freedom, Cherished Freedom

"What I like about cats is their independence, their want of gratitude and their indifference to prejudice, which allows them to descend without shame from the salon to the gutter," wrote François-René de Chateaubriand to his friend the Count de Marcellus, in an apt summation of the feline character.

As much as he dotes on his comfortable home and those who share it with him, he will always remain savage and evasive.

Because he has adapted himself completely to his life with man, people believe that he has suppressed all his animal instincts; but, as Dr. Michael Fox explains, "a domesticated cat is a savage animal that condescends to live with mankind, yet he has never subdued the tiger in his soul." It is exactly this duality in his nature that endows him with an intriguing aura of mystery.

Tame and savage, he is a denizen both of the salon and of the gutter.

In the salon, a pink ribbon tied around his neck, the cat leaps joyfully from one cushion to another and revels in the perfume of the Indian carnations his mistress has neatly arranged in the vases. As he parades ostentatiously from one place to another, you have the impression that the room was created around him, that it belongs to him. He knows every nook and corner better than anyone. He even forms his own opinion of the family's visitors, as often unfavorable as favorable.

Charles Baudelaire, in "Spleen et Idéal," wrote:

> He is the familial spirit of the household;
> He judges, presides, inspires
> All things in his empire;
> Could he be a sprite or a deity?

Whichever, at night he escapes through a half-open window and makes for the gutter. Nothing can stop him, not the luxury of the big armchair seemingly designed expressly for him, or the attentions lavished on him by his mistress, ever concerned with his welfare. He who cuts other cats dead in his living room or, at best, ignores them with icy indifference now hightails it for some gutter to join his circle of feline pals in their nightly rendezvous.

Solitary by day, at nightfall the apartment cat behaves like the gregarious, nocturnal alley cat he is. Aloof from his peers from morning to night, he joins them on equal terms when they gather together in some shadowy no-cat's-land to laze, sniff around, and rub their snouts. At the proper moment, they disperse, some to their family hearths, some to their rooftops, some to their alleys. No one has yet solved the enigma of these nighttime sessions, nor is it likely that anyone will in the foreseeable future.

Given his inscrutable character, it is no wonder that over the ages, various occult practitioners have designated the cat as the incarnate symbol of their credos. He lends himself altogether logically to their concepts of the supernatural.

Over the millennia he has been—and still is—the cynosure of contradictory prejudices, deified by some, detested by others. During that happy epoch when he ran after mice along the banks of the Nile, the Egyptians worshiped him as a god. Looking beyond his virtues as companion and aide, they were the first to invest him with such *noblesse* that he came to represent an ideal worthy of veneration for his enviable freedom, his strength and superiority over all other animals.

Thus exalted, his image was incorporated into the graceful figure of the cat-headed goddess Bast, who shared his conflicting traits of tenderness and serenity on the one hand, power and cruelty on the other. Born under the twin sign of the sun and the moon, she was put in celestial charge of light, warmth, and fecundity, also of mysterious darkness, the perils of night, and the omen of death. Sometimes she was seen clutching her brother's severed head in gory hands, as if to notify one and all that

Brigitte Mailliet: *Keeping Watch*

Magdalena Shummer: *Study in Green and Orange*

Gisèle Pierlot: *In a Garden*

Didier Richard: *Cold and Dreary*

behind her alluring charm she masked an ungodly taste for savagery.

In 59 B.C., a Roman official posted to Egypt discovered to his dismay the extent of the people's zealotry when he inadvertently killed a cat: they forthwith hanged him.

In that era when the cat was revered and feted as never before or since, he was embalmed in death and buried with ritual pomp worthy of a pharaoh; his mourners shaved off their eyebrows to show their grief. Ironically, when several hundred thousand cat mummies were uncovered during the excavations at Beni-Hasan, the inept archaeologists considered their find so trivial that they shipped twenty tons of them to England to be used as fertilizer at the bargain price of four pounds a ton.

At one time the core of Egypt's religious life, the cat achieved similar status in Japan. In the Orient, however, his career began badly. Of all the animals invited to attend Buddha's funeral, the cat was the only guest to arrive late. Worse yet, during the solemn rites, he allowed himself the thrill of chasing a rat, thus compounding the affront. Since one of Buddha's inviolable strictures forbade killing any living creature with deliberate intent, this gaffe landed him in the doghouse—the ultimate mortification—for centuries; but with the passage of time the Buddhist priests forgave him his impiety by tacit agreement, and restored him to respectability.

Despite his penchant for mischief-making, in time the feline spirit won the hearts of the Japanese. Few other countries, if any, can point with equal pride to their national cat shrines: temples dedicated to the cat and statues erected in his honor, often with one paw lifted to greet all comers and remind the forgetful to meditate.

The cat is buried in the cemetery of Gokoku-ji, built two centuries ago in Tokyo, where Buddhist monks chant hymns and pray for his soul's eternal rest.

While visiting the temple of Jichoin, Christian Marker, a French documentary filmmaker, lingered at length to watch the temple monks pray for all the cats in the world. He described the scene in these words:

A superb *maniki neko* (cat that salutes), mascot of merchants and prostitutes, stands guard at the gates of the sanctuary. For a small contribution, a temple priest will show you various cat statues. The oldest, dating back to the

Françoise Syx: *Ah, the Fragrance!*

Cellia Saubry: *The House of Cats*

sixteenth century, was donated by a warlord who, leading his army to the battlefield, saw his path blocked by a black cat. Instead of interpreting this as an evil omen, as many Westerners would do, he followed as the cat guided him to a strategic position so favorable that he won a resounding victory. Another temple, built in the seventeenth century, was contributed by a humble shopkeeper whose cat attracted such throngs of people gaping in wonder at its beauty that his business boomed and he amassed a fortune. Still another tribute, an eighteenth-century statue, was donated by a certain Belle Dame, whose identity no one knows. Did she own a cat she wished to immortalize or was Belle Dame a cat herself?

At both Gokoku-ji and Jichoin, the devout worshiped the cat in gratitude for the pleasure he gave them, and those with means dedicated costly tombs to his divinity to make sure that he would keep on replenishing their oversized coffers.

Apart from consecrating religious cults to the cat, the Japanese treasure him as an asset to their daily lives. In Japanese script, the ideogram for "cat" spells out his love of freedom.

If you visit the country, your Japanese friends will escort you to what amounts to a lay temple for cats called Neko-maya, also to a shop which sells only books on cats, pictures, cat cuisine and similar items. The first such emporium in the world, it has been emulated by Wholly Cats in San Francisco, Felines of Distinction in New York and The Sleeping Cat on the rue du Cherche Midi in Paris, next door to the florist. You may also learn how to pronounce the word *neko* and draw its ideogram: one bold stroke with two smaller ones, a plume for the tail, a rectangle with a cross to indicate a rice paddy (the Japanese associate the cat with rice paddies), and two small vertical strokes with a horizontal cross-bar, representing (not altogether comprehensibly to the foreigner) the feline nature, at once retiring and hot tempered.

But even though the cat has always claimed so many admirers all through his close association with mankind, just as many others, if not more, have feared and hated him, sometimes with such virulence that his fiercest enemies have put him to torture. According to popular tradition, witches are believed to have the

Marie-Hélène Véran: *Call of the Wild*

Madeleine Marcoux: *Treed*

Demonchy: *Cat Kingdom*

Françoise Syx: *A Washup in the Strawberry Patch*

power to turn themselves into cats at will; legend tells us of eerie, howling corteges accompanying cat-witches through dark forests on windy, moonless nights on the way to their orgiastic rituals.

Countless times over the centuries, superstitious notions have driven the cat's foes to commit brutal atrocities against the species, no doubt in the belief that by so doing they were exorcising evil spirits in the interests of improving their life-style. The live cat has been burned on the pyre, thrown from lofty towers, or drowned, thus paying with his life for the hatred his independence has cost him. Moreover, in the past, church authorities forbade all cat cults and excommunicated the animal as a tool of Satan, if not—given his black coat—Satan himself.

Enigmatic, withdrawn into a world of his own, the cat unwittingly fosters the credulity of the gullible and the collective hysteria of fanatics, to serve as an ill-fated catalyst in sabbatical rites, often enlivened by the poppy and hashish.

Although he has regained his rightful place in modern, more enlightened civilization, he is yet persistently thought to be the herald of omens, good or bad, depending on what you believe. Even today, a superstitious pedestrian will ward off bad luck by crossing the street when he sees a black cat in his path (black in the United States and France, white elsewhere).

More than any other sector of the population, firemen are justified in cursing imprudent cats. Statistics show that they give more headaches to firemen than to any other segment of the population.

In his love of freedom, the cat will scale the most inaccessible heights—the summit of a steep, sloping roof or the uppermost branch of a towering tree.

Then, petrified, the wretched creature will not budge from his perilous perch. Losing his customary haughty poise, he meows piteously. Far below, shops empty of their customers and traffic is halted as crowds of onlookers swarm into the street, clucking their tongues in commiseration. The cat's distraught mistress shrieks in desperation and flings her arms about. Bright red fire engines come clanging to the scene with a deafening clamor. The firemen raise their long ladder and risk life and limb to rescue him, verbalizing their sentiments in unprintable language.

When the wayward cat is finally returned, trembling, to the custody of his mistress, he gradually recovers his cool in her comforting arms. Back in the security of home, he washes him-

Jehanne Jouvenaud: *The Suitors*

Christine Cipriano: *Tom, Miette, and Blue Iris*

Christine Cipriano: *Birds and Blue Skies*

Anne-Marie Sabatier: *Firemen to the Rescue!*

self all over to lift his spirits, then, with consummate dignity, crawls into his private turf, such as the narrow space between two potted plants, to sleep off his terrifying misadventure and erase it from his mind—and woe to anyone who dares to disturb him.

Every cat cohabiting with other cats in one ménage will choose his favorite nook and guard it jealously against all potential raiders. On the other hand, once claims have been settled to the satisfaction of all, he will never intrude where he is not welcome. Unclaimed areas, however, will be accessible to everyone.

The cat is at once a sociable animal and a loner. When he hunts, pretends to sleep but listens for the faintest sound, or plays, he neither needs nor wants company. Self-reliant, intelligent, and bursting with vitality, he is well able to manage his own affairs without any assistance.

A unique factor of man's genius is his capacity to apply acquired knowledge and skills to almost any eventuality. Thus, in the United States we find psychiatrists who specialize in treating cats with jumpy nerves. Some people, worried about their maladjusted cats, entrust them into the care of analysts for weekly sessions at terrifying fees.

Which of the two is sicker, cat or man?

Often kindness and attention will cure a neurotic kitten taken into a strange environment at too early an age. A congenial home and companionship will help him overcome his neurosis and adjust to the prospect of a solitary future better than any psychotherapist could do. The root of all a cat's woes is the lack of human understanding and sympathy.

Some people expect cats to behave like canines; hence they try to train their kitten like a puppy, unaware that this will cause him mental distress or, what's worse, deny him the essence of his cathood. They fail to understand that a cat will never bestow his graces on command; it is he who decides whether he loves you or not, how much, and when he wants to demonstrate his affection.

In *Dynasties blanches et noires*, Théophile Gautier, who presided over a virtual menagerie, wrote:

Winning a cat's friendship is not simple. He is a peaceful, philosophical, methodical animal attached to his habits, to order and cleanliness. He does not grant his good will easily. If you are worthy of his affection, he will be your friend, but

Cellia Saubry: *By the Light of the Full Moon*

Anne-Marie Sabatier: *On the Roofs*

Fanny Darnat: *The Wrong Side of the Tracks*

never your slave. He will never belie his instincts nor will he do anything he considers unreasonable, even though he loves you. But if he gives himself to you, it will always be with complete trust and loyalty.

Cats fascinated Gilbert Ganne, who devoted many pages to them in his *Orgueil de la maison* exactly because they are so distant and different:

> For me, this is one of a cat's most endearing attractions: He never pretends to give himself to you or to be anything other than what he is, however strong his bond with you may be. This is why cats so often offend people's sensitivities and why they are so little appreciated. He will always be true to his species.

You must accept a cat on his own terms with love and tolerance for his brusque changes of mood. You must also realize that he is different from all other domestic animals because he is always fully in possession of his indomitable self. This is his strength and the source of his mystery. How can we begrudge him his uncompromising demand for freedom of thought and action when every one of us aspires, however vainly, to achieve this same ideal condition?

At night, when the moon rises and the cat goes forth in search of adventure, all destinations are equally inviting—Kipling's Wet Wild Woods, a clump of bushes, a lookout high up on some deserted roof, wherever chance leads him.

Scrounging to find a scintillating star at the bottom of a trash can or dreaming of luscious birds in flight, at once prince and beggar, the cat is all magic.

The Eyes of Night

Since time immemorial, cats' eyes have always held a powerful fascination for people, especially artists, sages, lovers, and witches. How do you account for it?

Cats, it is generally believed, can see through the darkest shadows of night. This unique attribute is somehow related to the irresistible attraction you feel for him when he turns his wide, unblinking orbs on you, as if to penetrate the secrets of your innermost thoughts.

Because he is a hunter by instinct, the world at night is his realm. Endowed by nature with a visual capacity so acute that he can detect the faintest vestige of light, he will roam wherever his whim guides him in the black hours between sunset and dawn.

When the light is strong, his pupils contract to a barely visible slit, but enlarge as they adjust to pierce the densest curtain of night.

So say the experts; but this simplistic explanation fails to satisfy the cat-lover. Cats' eyes, he will say, cannot be subjected to laboratory research, because they defy all rational analysis. This is one aspect of his inimitable self.

Nor should the poet allow his imagination to soar too high when he describes his cat's haunting gaze in verse: he must understand that behind the nuances of light reflected in his pet's eyes lies the revelation of his soul.

When he expresses fear, if the pupils contract in normal daylight, you can tell that he senses an imminent attack. If they dilate, he is preparing to defend himself before the enemy seizes

64

the advantage. When, turned into himself, he lowers his eyelids as if to draw a veil over his most intimate thoughts, you can be sure that he is experiencing some pleasurable sensation, the memory of a caress, perhaps, or the warmth of the sun. When he wishes to convey a message to you, he communicates in his fashion, with eager eyes and pointed ears. If you catch him glaring at another cat, he is telling a would-be raider to shove off: this is his territory.

Such are the conclusions drawn by animal psychologists after long study. But the facts they uncovered had already been known to poets of vision.

Charles Baudelaire, for one. In his verses, Baudelaire, whose affinity with cats was so strong that he never failed to win their devotion on first acquaintance—he could stroke a strange cat the wrong way without so much as a scratch to show for it— eloquently foretold what researchers would take years to discover.

In one of three sonnets dedicated to cats, the poet lifted a veil and told us something new about the odd look in their eyes:

THE CATS

Lovers, scholars—the fervent, the austere—
grow equally fond of cats, their household pride.
As sensitive as either to the cold,
as sedentary, though so strong and sleek,

Your cat, a friend to learning and to love,
seeks out both silence and the awesome dark.
Hell would have made the cat its courier
could it have controverted feline pride.

Dozing, all cats assume the svelte design
of desert sphinxes sprawled in solitude,
apparently transfixed by endless dreams;
their teeming loins are rich in magic sparks

And golden specks like infinitesimal sand
glisten in those enigmatic eyes.

(translated by Richard Howard)

Cats' eyes drew an awed response from the ancients, who demonstrated their admiration through actions rather than

Brigitte Mailliet: *Portrait of Lilac*

Marie-Hélène Véran: *In the Country*

Zofia Szalowska: *Mona Feline*

Françoise Syx: *The Magic Garden*

Brigitte Mailliet: *My Friend Under the Stars*

words. By offering them shelter at nightfall, the Egyptians spanned the hours between sundown and sunrise: for the brilliance of their eyes, they prized cats as guardians of precious light.

On the other side of the globe, meanwhile, the Chinese breathed life into their cat statues by illuminating the empty eyes with glowing lamps.

Emerald, phosphorescent, a cat's eyes wield hypnotic power.

In past centuries, on the night of Mardi Gras, frightened peasants barricaded themselves behind closed shutters, swearing that they could hear cats howling with the wolves. And to whom, the peasants asked, if not to Lucifer himself?

"Only imbeciles do not know that all cats are committed to a binding contract with the Devil," asserts the Gospel of the Devil.

Witches donned castoff cat skins to ride their brooms to their midnight orgies, celebrated to propitiate the Fates and win their benevolence. The center of these demoniacal soirées was the sacrificial cat consigned to the pyre, where the light of his extinguished eyes was replaced by glowing flames.

Like the narrator of Edgar Allan Poe's horror tale "The Black Cat," many naïve souls believed that all you had to do to solve a cat's mystery, and thereby evade his malevolent influence, was rid yourself of his eyes and of him. Poe's cat was a

remarkably large and beautiful animal, entirely black and sagacious to an astonishing degree. In speaking of his intelligence, my wife, who at heart was not a little tinctured with superstition, made frequent allusions to the ancient popular notion, which regarded all cats as witches. . . .

Pluto—this was the cat's name—was my favorite pet and playmate. I alone fed him, and he attended me wherever I went about the house. It was even with difficulty that I could prevent him from following me through the streets.

Our friendship lasted, in this manner, for several years, during which my general temperament and character— through the instrumentality of the Fiend Intemperance— had (I blush to confess) experienced a radical alteration for the worse. I grew, day by day, more moody, more irritable, more regardless of the feelings of others. I suffered myself to use intemperate language to my wife. At length, I even offered her personal violence. . . . But my disease grew upon

Bernard Partiot: *Find the Cat in the Tree*

Odile Gaillard: *Felines*

odile gaillard

me—for what disease is like Alcohol!—and at length even Pluto, who was now becoming old, and consequently somewhat peevish—even Pluto began to experience the effects of my ill temper.

One night, returning home much intoxicated from one of my haunts about town, I fancied that the cat avoided my presence. I seized him; when, in his fright at my violence, he inflicted a slight wound upon my hand with his teeth. The fury of a demon instantly possessed me. I knew myself no longer. My original soul seemed, at once, to take its flight from my body; and a more than fiendish malevolence, gin-nurtured, thrilled every fibre of my frame. I took from my waistcoat-pocket a penknife, opened it, grasped the poor beast by the throat, and deliberately cut one of its eyes from the socket! I blush, I burn, I shudder, while I pen the damnable atrocity.

Thus sacrificed to the narrator's ungovernable rage, Pluto is reincarnated into another black cat (who says the cat doesn't have nine lives?), with a white spot on his breast, which grows little by little into the macabre form of a gibbet. Let no one think he can escape a cat's evil eye!

But, happily, he is not always pledged to witchcraft. Indeed, in societies all over the world, legend presents him more as a herald of good luck than a tiresome troublemaker.

For example: you really shouldn't bury a live cat in your wheat field, of course, but if you do, you can count on a bountiful crop at harvest time. Or if you immure him in the wall of the new cottage you're building, he'll not only bring you great fortune but will also make sure your daughter will marry the man she's been using every wile at her command to rope in.

In Charles Perrault's fable "Puss-in-Boots," the puss in question, a crafty type, intrigues to promote his humble young master, son of a poor, simple miller, to the exalted status of a nobleman, with the fancy title of Marquis de Carabas. Puss achieves this remarkable feat by conniving to expropriate the castle belonging to an ogre as well as all his vast domain. Not only that, he even manages to marry the fellow off to none other than the daughter of the king. Here's how he did it:

Puss-in-Boots arrived at the residence of a very rich ogre,

Thérèse Coustry: *Cat Caught on a Cold Chimney*

Agnès Emanuelli: *Zen at Ease*

Zofia Szalowska: *Green Eyes*

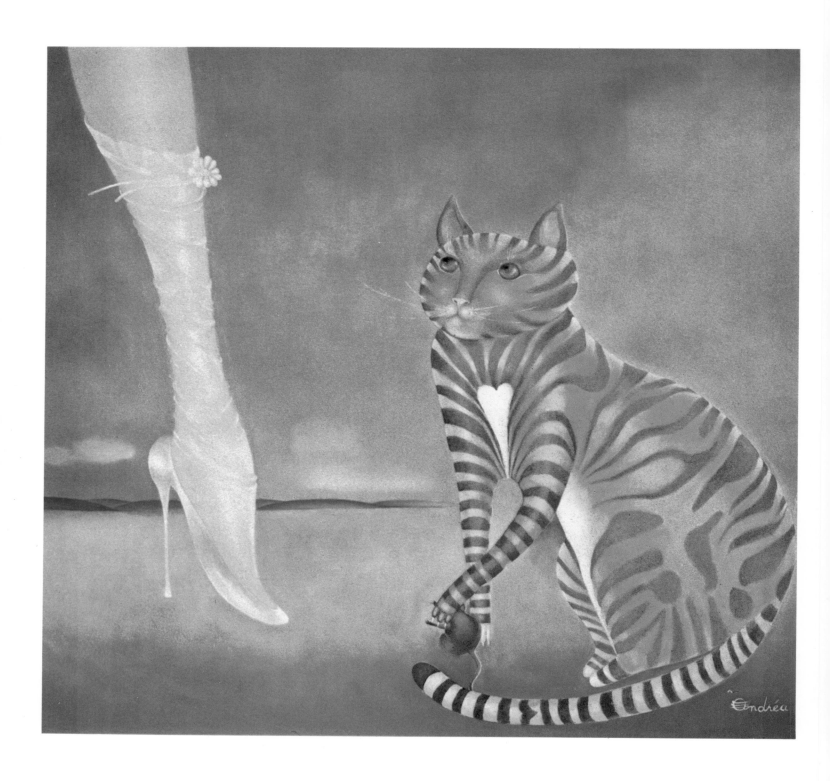

Andréa Emery: *The Gift*

who owned all these possessions. The cat wished to know who this ogre was and what he was able to do, so he asked to speak with him, saying that he could not pass so near to his castle without paying him reverence.

The ogre received him very civilly and offered him a bed to rest in.

"I have been assured, sire," the cat said after his repose, "that you can change yourself into any kind of beast—a lion, say, or an elephant."

"That is true," replied the ogre curtly. "You will see me turned into a lion."

When Puss-in-Boots beheld a lion before him, he fled to the roof and only descended when the ogre resumed his natural guise.

"I vow," said Puss, "that you gave me a terrible fright. I have also been assured," he went on, "but find it difficult to believe, that you can take the form of the smallest animal, like a rat or a mouse. I'm sure that's altogether impossible."

"Impossible!" exclaimed the ogre. "You shall see." And as he spoke, he transformed himself into a mouse and scurried across the floor. No sooner did Puss perceive this than he threw himself on the mouse and ate him up.

Meanwhile, the king, who was passing by, observed the ogre's fine castle and wished to see it inside. The cat ran to him and cried, "You Majesty is most welcome to the castle of the Marquis of Carabas."

Now then, if you consider Puss-in-Boots to be, above all, a loyal friend, you will also admit that he combines intelligence with a hunter's skill, which he has put at the service of his master. This is his singular way of thanking him for all the good things he has bestowed on him. Was he, after all, so cruel, this cat, in getting rid of the ogre-mouse to reciprocate all his master's kindnesses?

Not at all. His was a commendable act of gratitude toward an honest youth who had the good sense to love a cat with all his

Annie Rétivat: *Portrait of an Unknown Woman*

Annie Rétivat: *The Stranger*

heart. If anyone thinks otherwise, this argument should fully justify Puss-in-Boots's unorthodox method of procedure.

"Black god and blond devil," magician and sorcerer with a twinkle in his eye, the cat leaves to us humans the complicated task of figuring him out.

Let us now contemplate the startling affinity that parallels feline carnality with the sensuality that characterizes the female of the human species. This analogy was first made public four thousand years ago at Bubastis in Egypt, when all good Egyptians worshiped the deity Bast, consort of the sun-god Ra.

The Egyptians revered the cat for the nobility of his features, his unorthodoxy, and his enviable almond-shaped eyes. His beauty, sometimes enhanced by a gold ring in his ear, encompassed all the graces of womankind. The similarities are striking: his sleek fur (in Charlemagne's time, cat skin cost more than sable) and her silken hair; the supple frame and elastic step; natural elegance and a depth of feeling you see when one or the other gazes at you amorously. In those days, Egyptian women applied a touch of kohl to accentuate their eyes, imitating the cat's elongated orbs. Women everywhere are still doing it today.

The similarity, however, goes below the surface; it exists in a woman's inner being, which, disguised like a cat's, is the very essence of herself. The same voluptuousness that motivates a cat, a creature made for love, allies him with the woman intent on making the most of her dual role in life as mistress and mother.

This kindred spirit intensifies a woman's image, her mysterious charm, and her powers of seduction (not to mention the perversities they induce).

Few poets have limned this invisible bond as aptly as Baudelaire. "I confounded cat scent with the scent of the female," he wrote in one of his intimate journals; and when he saw his cat gazing at him, he also saw the disquieting image of the woman he loved. Because she was no less secretive and sensual than his pet, Baudelaire at once venerated and feared her.

THE CAT

Come, my beautiful creature, sheathe your claws,
Rest on my amorous heart,
And let me plunge into your marvelous eyes
Of mingled metal and agate.

Gisèle Pierlot: *The Clairvoyant*

Agnès Godard: *Rendezvous at Night*

Sophie Sirot: *An Unhappy Encounter*

Patricia de Breuvery: *Two in One*

Didier Richard: *The Temple of Cats*

Marta Gaspar: *The Dreamer*

When my fingers caress at leisure
Your supple, elastic back
And my hand tingles with pleasure
From your body's electric contact,

I seem to see my mistress. Her regard,
Like yours, nice animal,
Deep and cold,
Cuts and thrusts like a sword.

And from her feet to her head's dark coronal
A subtle air, a dangerous perfume
Swim round her brown body's dusty bloom.

(translated by Doreen Bellen)

The cat-woman of fable has left so marked an impression on cultures everywhere in the world that she figures prominently in the folklore of many races, particularly in Asia, where the cat has won himself a position of preeminence.

One of the most popular heroines of Japanese legend is the seductive but cruel witch-cat Bake Neko, who makes it her business to invade private homes disguised as a harmless, gentle puss. But children, beware! With one sudden, agile bound, she will hurl herself onto a naughty brat who refuses to obey his elders and make a meal of him.

Incongruously, in this sophisticated age of nuclear technology, she still inspires Japanese authors and poets with her uncommon escapades. Brought up to date, Bake Neko is the protagonist of a television series that has achieved wide popularity with the Japanese public.

The following comments were made by Christian Marker after a recent visit to the Land of the Rising Sun:

I don't know how many films have been made with Bake Neko as the leading character. The story is always the same: a man is murdered; a cat, witness to the assassination, transmogrifies his spirit into the body of a young woman; and whatever version you see, there will always be a scene in which she takes on feline gestures, such as clawing the air with her paw or lapping up liquids with her tongue instead of drinking them. This woman, then, becomes the instrument of revenge, so enthralling that the spectators even

Arlette Laville: *Waiting*

Zofia Szalowska: *Angry Cat*

André-Yves Fey: *Gods of the Nile*

Setsuko Uno: *Curiosity*

Christian Sylvain: *Those Far Away Hills*

forget their taste for saké wine. But typically in these films, her vengeance, at first conforming to the Japanese code of morals, goes out of control. Unleashed fury falls on innocent persons, blood flows freely and the cat-woman meets a brutal death, her decapitated head flying over rooftops. But like Dr. Jekyll and the invisible man, she will reappear in the next episode.

Fables told in ancient lands as far apart as Greece and Japan have to do with cats that turned into women. In a story by Marie-Catherine d'Aulnoy, a prince is deeply touched by the graceful bearing of "the most beautiful white cat that ever lived," whose "meows, so soft and charming," go "straight to his heart." For the passion she awakens in him, her divine form undergoes a metamorphosis, from which she emerges as a woman with an equally divine body. In Greek lore, a she-cat enamored of a man petitions Venus to transform her into a woman; her plea is granted, but, unable to suppress her feline instincts, she persists in chasing mice—a sport hardly suitable to a royal princess.

On the other hand, people can be changed into cats. Such a fate befell two Japanese lovers as punishment for committing the unspeakable crime of eloping. This sort of thing was simply not done in old Japan.

A popular French tale, "La Chatte de la Croix de Haies," is a bedtime story, told only when nature provides sighing winds and other nocturnal sound effects. Fernand Méry recounts it in his book on cats:

One night, Father Pichard was returning from Haute-Chapelle, whither he had gone to court the woman who would soon become his wife, when he spied a she-cat huddled at the foot of the crucifix known as the Cross of Haies, which stands at the crossroads. She was a big, white, love-sick cat, rubbing her legs and meowing. For a long time thereafter, every evening he found her at the very same spot. Then he married Nanon, his fiancée. Months passed and he forgot the cat. But one night he woke with a start, to find that he was all alone: his beautiful Nanon was gone. Pichard thought this very strange, especially when he opened his eyes in the early dawn and discovered that Nanon had quietly slipped back into bed.

Pichard asked her questions, which she refused to answer.

Marie-Hélène Véran: *On the Banks of the Nile*

Marie-Hélène Véran: *Egyptian Goddess*

André-Yves Fey: *Arctic Adventure*

Valentin Marcq: *He Who Likes Flowers*

Zofia Szalowska: *The Magician*

He grew angry, threatened her and sulked. That evening he lay beside her in bed, as always. At midnight, however, again he awoke and saw that his wife was missing. But on the floor near him, there was the white cat, purring. She was still there the next morning. And thus it was every night that followed. Now, the door was always firmly bolted; how, then, did the she-cat enter the room? Intrigued, Pichard determined to keep watch. He never heard his wife depart, but one night he saw a white paw come out of a small hole as it reached for the bolt. . . . He quietly rose from the bed, grasped his axe and cut off the offending paw.

For eight days he saw no trace of Nanon. When she finally returned home, her head lowered, her complexion blotched, she encountered her husband without a word of greeting. Instead, she wept with shame because her hand had been lopped off at the wrist.

One of the most ancient of all cat fables is "Beauty and the Beast," which dates back to early Indian mythology and appears in various versions in many countries. In a French version by Marie Leprince de Beaumont, the Beast is half-man, half-cat, desperately in love with Beauty, whom he detains in his castle. Like Bake Neko, he is imbued with human emotions, but he cannot always repress his savage impulses. Thus, when a gazelle skips across the garden, Beast cannot resist the temptation to chase it. When, smeared with blood, he returns to Beauty and looks at her, she sees her image mirrored in his eyes and thereby discovers her true self.

A cat reveals his traits through his eyes. In his shifting moods, now he is gentle, now wise, cunning, serene, or violent; and if we look into them hard enough, like Beauty, we too shall discover our true selves.

The Eternal Feline

Let a cat cross a room, even the most humble, and he will invest it with the quiet intimacy of a boudoir. Yet it is not the room, however rich and tasteful, that lends its charm to the cat, but the other way around. He creates an aura in which (in the words of Charles Baudelaire) "All is order and beauty,/Luxury, tranquillity and voluptuousness."

Undulating silent and majestic, never does he collide with the furniture or topple some fragile bibelot and send it crashing to the floor, as some clumsy canine will do. His very presence will transform the most unpretentious corner into an enchanted nook the moment he sets a pink paw in it.

He re-creates the backdrop nature intended for him: a sumptuous Egyptian palace, the ebony and mother-of-pearl of a plush Napoleon III armchair, or the gold tassels and red velvet upholstery of a Victorian divan, where he can curl up and drop off to sleep in a setting that befits him.

In the Victorian era, in fact, the English acquired something of a cat mania and, especially among the well-to-do, a cat figure became an indispensable item in drawing-room decor. In his book *Le Chat dans tous ses États*, Jean-Louis Hue describes this nineteenth-century parlor:

> The house cat was an invention of the nineteenth century. In France and England he lent the ultimate touch of perfection to the domestic scene—a tufted jungle with its crowded array of sofas, love seats, Oriental poufs, pot-bellied com-

modes and Gallé glassware trailing translucent ivy, the whole stuffy room suffused in a bilious green or violet light. The porcelain cat, an indispensable item of decoration, stood or sat in its proper place. If the lady of the house detected the smallest speck of foreign matter on his ceramic coat, horrified she summoned the housemaid to come at once and remove it with her turkey-feather duster.

On the walls hung portraits of dear, but dreary, cats, painted by contemporary artists of dubious talents. Cat collars, out of fashion, were replaced by a pink or baby-blue ribbon tied into a fetching bow at his throat. The animals posed crouching decorously under a fringed lampshade or watching, with adorable curiosity, the brass pendulum of a grandfather clock swinging to and fro. Sometimes the cat blended harmoniously into a display of peonies or other gaudy flowers.

The sixteenth-century French poet Joachim du Bellay, inconsolable after the death of his adored she-cat, memorialized her in these touching verses:

> That was Belaud, my little gray cat,
> Belaud, who was, by my good fortune,
> The most beautiful work of art that nature
> Ever made of any cat.
> That was Belaud, death to rats,
> Whose surpassing splendor
> Merits immortality.
>
> Small snout, tiny teeth,
> Eyes that shone not too bright,
> Yet the blue-green pupils
> Reflected the color spectrum
> Of a rainbow
> Arched across the sky.
> Head perfectly proportioned,
> Neck plump, ears short,
> A little leonine muzzle
> Sprouting a silver beard
> With a tuft of downy hair,
> She had the face of a young demoiselle,
> A throat delicate and sweet,
> A tail as long as a monkey's,
> Spotted by nature's pigmentation.

Zofia Szalowska: *Rousseau*

Magdalena Shummer: *Beneath the Roses*

Maria de Posz: *Simona*

> That was Belaud, a gentle thing
> Endowed with such beauty
> From head to foot
> That never has her peer been seen.

More than likely, grief deranged the poet to some extent—but then, the loved one who leaves us behind is always unlike any other living thing, always irreplaceable, always superior; we forget his less-than-endearing, even exasperating, traits and habits. Deep sorrow can engender excessive emotions and, as in the case of du Bellay, fustian poetry.

On a cold winter night, Cendra Vernaz, a writer, offered shelter to Kor, a stray cat, who thenceforth became her constant companion. As they warmed themselves by the fire, Kor told her a story:

At the beginning of time, the male of the human race had not yet acquired a name; this was the penalty meted out to him as punishment for his destructive impulses. He was desperate; without a proper noun to identify him, his position in the world could never be secure. His female counterpart, not at all inclined to make mayhem of other living things, hence wiser than he, had long since acquired a name: Woman.

When he lamented his misfortune to her, Woman advised him that he could resolve his dilemma by ascertaining which animal was the most beautiful in all the world. "Go forth," she said, "explore the animal kingdom and find him. But mark you: leave your bow and arrow behind."

Taking her advice, he set out and met in turn a hippopotamus, a giraffe, a turtle, and a polecat. One told him to find the slimmest, another the smallest, another the most agile, and lastly the sweetest smelling. Fearful that such a task was beyond his limited capacity, he continued on his way. All at once he met an animal he had never seen before, and addressed him:

"What is your name, you whom I do not know?"

"Ah, but I know you, and I also know what you're looking for: the most beautiful animal in all the world."

"That's right. But I am weary and my mind is confused. I don't know where to turn."

"In such matters," said the animal, "I'm an expert. By the way, let me introduce myself. I'm the cat. Now then…let's put your

Susan Tantlinger: *Fafa*

Madeleine Marcoux: *Blue Mood*

Magdalena Shummer: *Among the Lilies-of-the-Valley*

Susan Tantlinger: *The Big, Black Tom*

thoughts in order. What did that fat, ugly hippopotamus tell you?''

"He said I must look for the slimmest animal in the realm," the stranger replied after a moment's reflection.

"Good. Look at me. Am I not the slimmest?" the cat said, and stretched himself out to display his slender figure and enviable profile. "Then which beast did you meet? Try to remember."

"I think it was the giraffe. He told me to look for the smallest."

"That one, all legs and neck," the cat commented with a hint of disdain. "Well, don't you see that I am the smallest?" And he clung to the bark of a baobab tree with his four claws so that the stranger could admire his fine proportions at their best. "There, you see. I'm slim and small."

Sitting hunched over on a rock, the stranger sat up to get a better look. "Yes, I suppose you are," he said. "Now I'm beginning to think more clearly. If I'm not mistaken, I met the turtle next."

"Wise, but awfully slow. What did he suggest?"

"That I must know which is the most agile of animals."

"He rises in my estimation," said the cat. "I'll pay my compliments next time I see him. Now, watch me."

Thrice he leapt forward and thrice backward, each time turning around in midair before landing squarely on his paws. Then he arched his back and drew his paws together so that you couldn't tell which belonged in front and which behind. Then he sat down. "What animal," he asked, "could be more agile than I am?"

"I can see," replied the stranger, "that you are slim, small, and agile. But there's one more thing—"

"I know what that stinking polecat had to say," the cat interrupted huffily. "For once he's been honest about his loathsome stench. You'll see that I'm the sweetest smelling of all."

With that, he climbed up on the rock and reclined gracefully at the stranger's side. "Now, stroke my back from ears to tail. Does my fur reek like those foul-smelling skins you wrap around yourself to keep warm in winter? Can you feel a single malodorous weed or rotting bit of moss? You do not. My odor is faint and pleasing to the nose. That's because I take scrupulous care of my personal hygiene. I'm different from all other animals because I *wash* myself."

He began to lick his forepaws, first the right one toe by toe and, if you please, between the toes, then the left paw. That

Christine Cipriano: *Blanchette*
Christine Cipriano: *Griselda*

Christine Cipriano: *Mistigri*

Christine Cipriano: *Domino*

Zofia Szalowska: *Hortense*

Z. Szałowska 81

done, he bathed his face, the right cheek with his left paw, and vice versa.

"I won't clean my ears today," he explained, "because if I do, it's sure to rain."

Instead he carefully licked his flanks all the way down to his underbelly and nibbled at his hind paws. The stranger looked on in amazement. "I have never seen any creature take so much care to keep himself clean—including myself," he thought, vexed, then asked aloud, "How many times a month do you go to all this trouble?"

"A month! Every day, of course," the cat replied, haughtily, "and sometimes twice a day."

"In that case," the stranger said, "I pronounce you the most beautiful animal in all the world."

He returned to Woman and told her of his decision. Hardly had he finished speaking when he heard a disembodied voice, which seemed to come from heaven.

"You're right," the voice thundered, rolling the *rs*, "and for your wisdom and good taste, henceforth your name shall be Man."

Leonardo da Vinci once declared that "the small feline is a masterpiece"; and the philosopher Émile-Auguste Chartier, known as Alain, maintained that "there are two things aesthetically perfect in the world: the bell and the cat."

Ever since the cat came into his own thousands of years ago in Egypt, he has provided painters and sculptors with an endless source of inspiration. He appears repeatedly in the genre paintings of the seventeenth-century Flemish masters, also in the works of Tintoretto, Ghirlandaio, and other great artists, among them Boucher, Chardin, Courbet, Géricault, Renoir, Bonnard, Picabia, Picasso, Foujita, Balthus, and Léonor Fini, to mention only a few. Even longer is the roster of naïve painters who posed him prominently in their works.

By placing him at the model's feet in his masterpiece *Olympia*, Édouard Manet associated the cat with ideal beauty. In his portrayal of the two figures, the woman's magnolia-tinted flesh is effectively set off by the black fur of the cat, whose languid pose underscores her persuasive allure.

Although so many artists have chosen the cat as the symbol of beauty, unfortunately he is too often enslaved by this asset— as when less discerning souls feel the need to gather their

Patricia de Breuvery: *Unexpected Visit*

Mimi Vang Olsen: *Hatshepsut at the Window*

Christine Cipriano: *Blue Eyes*

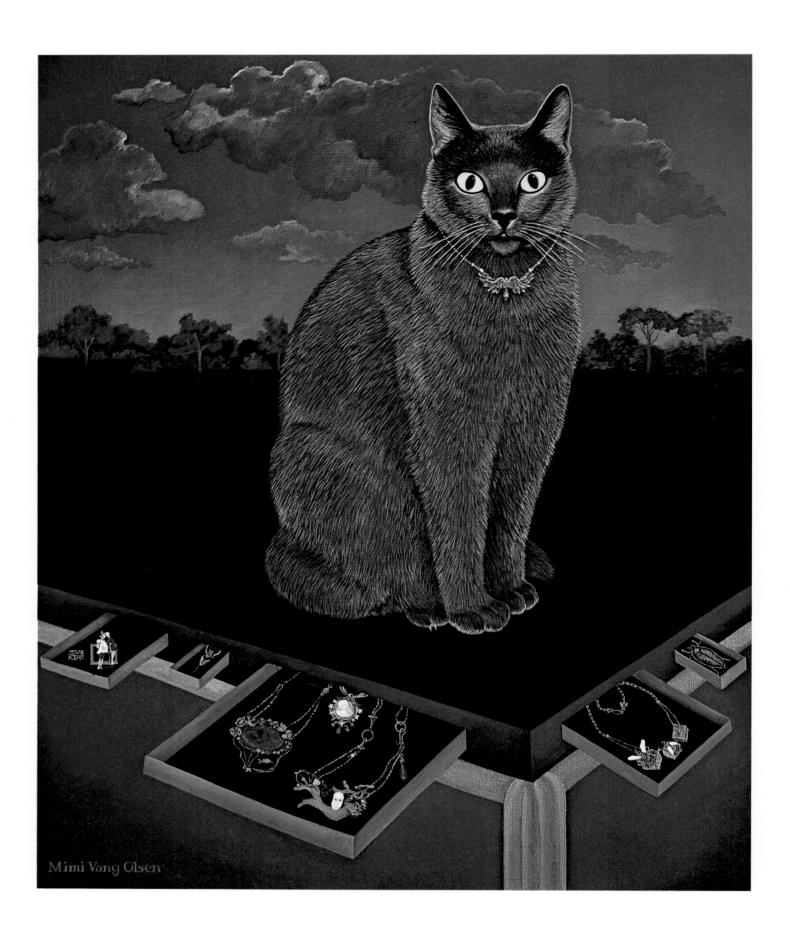

Mimi Vang Olsen: *Cartier*

Mimi Vang Olsen: *Gray Cat on a Pink Cushion*

pets together once a year to compare their good points in competitions.

Brushed to a glossy sheen, weighed and minutely inspected, the victorious show cat captures the first prize only after long and patient preparations. Tough judges consulting their rule books, pen in hand, are ready to pounce on the smallest imperfection— a hair out of place, an overlong snout, or a claw too short—to disqualify an otherwise exemplary contestant.

Can physical beauty be measured by any rigid set of standards? Not at all. At best, you can determine the purity of an animal's breed, but beauty is an abstract quality that submits to no rule of thumb. It emanates from the cat like a subtle whiff of perfume.

Sometimes the cat's beauty is exploited for commercial purposes. Ever since the last century, when manufacturers took to hawking their wares in advertising campaigns, they have imposed upon the feline image to extol the merits of their products. In this era of consumerism, the cat is a commodity not only to be bought and sold but also—an offense to his dignity— to promote trade.

Thus, his soft, silent tread is just the thing to endorse rubber-soled footwear; the sheen of his fur testifies to the high vitamin content of certain prepared foods; a given brand of fuel will keep you as warm and cozy as a cat reclining in front of a blazing fireplace; and the carriage trade will rush to Madison Avenue or the rue de la Paix to snap up luxury items that betoken the cat's hedonistic tastes.

He is also a profitable asset to the film industry. The comic hero of numerous animated cartoons and a leading player in long and short films, the cat has made a significant contribution to cinematic art. A confirmed scene-stealer, he has delighted moviegoers who have seen him nestled in Audrey Hepburn's arms, keeping Kim Novak company, providing the motive for a lively spat between Jean Gabin and Simone Signoret, and in other cameo roles. Some feline thespians have even distinguished themselves as winners of the Patsy, the Oscar equivalent for the best movie performance of the year given by an actor from the animal kingdom.

Thus, the cat participates in human affairs as high priest, artist's model, film actor, and, of more immediate concern to the distaff side, as beauty consultant to women who would like to improve their appearance and fend off the telltale marks of advancing age.

Sprawling lazily in a dresser drawer amid an array of silks,

Simone Castex: *Pompon in Majesty*

Christine Cipriano: *Posing with Clouds*

Christine Cipriano: *Only Feathers for My Trouble*

dainty underthings, and flacons of perfume, he suggests ideas whereby a woman can transform herself into a Lorelei, if that is her aspiration. Observing herself in him as if in a mirror and charmed by the vision, she can pick up a few hints, such as giving her eyes the look of a silent movie vamp.

For the figure, he recommends a daily workout. Setting a good example, he revives himself with a hasty exercise routine. First, he stretches himself flat on the floor, hind paws as far as they will go, and yawns so wide to relax his jaws that you wonder if something might not snap. Now he gets to his feet and extends his body, torso round and tail standing straight as a fakir's rope. Too much exercise, however, is not good for you, so the cat leaves off and sits down to begin his morning toilette.

His first tongue-licks came from his mother just after he emerged from her womb, covered with a viscous placenta. The sensation pleased him so much that he has been doing it himself ever since during much of his waking hours. He flattens a cowlick here, slaps down a flea there, polishes somewhere else, then dusts off his breast, shoulders, and back. His ultimate aim is to find some way of licking under the chin, but thus far he hasn't made it. Resting on one side, he probes his stomach, pinches a bump on the ilium, lifts a paw, and licks it from bottom to top like a lollipop. He never overlooks the smallest detail. If something itches, he licks it again and again until it goes away. Now doubled up, he cleans up his tail or combs out a clump of hair he can untangle only with his teeth. Remembering his crop, he smooths it down against his neck; the bouffant style is not for him.

To make the most of her physical assets, any woman would do well to follow his example.

Brigitte Mailliet: *Portrait of Sikkim* (a detail)

Lord
of the
Manor

What's the difference between a household that includes a cat and one that doesn't? At a glance, nothing. All living rooms have their quota of sofas, chairs, coffee tables, and lamps; all bedrooms their beds, dressers, boudoir chairs, and closets. So what is the difference? you ask. Answer: If you take a good look around, you'll find that nothing is the same.

Primarily, a cat is the "visible soul" of the ménage, as Jean Cocteau put it. Which is self-explanatory.

Otherwise, for one thing, he has pressed so often against the wall of his corner of the room to wash himself and wax his moustache that the white paint has noticeably turned gray. Moreover, by spending a good deal of his time there and impregnating it with his odor, he has conspicuously designated it as totally his.

Elsewhere, he has worked his claws over the armrests of the sofa, ignoring his mistress's "Don't scratch" dictum. On the sofa's expanse he leaves tiny strands of white hair so visible that you can almost count them, vestiges of a cozy nap some unwelcome disturbance has interrupted.

Again, to please his own special taste, he will recompose the tiger lilies his mistress has arranged with her customary loving care in a long-necked vase, or redesign the plants with his teeth to make them look more like the lotus leaves that bordered the Nile so many ages ago and that continue to haunt his memory.

Now he perches himself atop the bookshelves, his four paws lined up at the edge, his tail wrapped around him, to survey his handiwork. He blinks at the scene, pleased with the improvements his artistic skill has achieved, then extends his torso, takes an acrobatic leap, and lands in a cardboard box below, where he contracts himself to fit comfortably into it. With his head hunched between his shoulders and his paws tucked under him, he drops off to sleep.

A deep sleep, by all appearances; but in fact he is keeping a constant watch over the premises in total silence, not like that ill-mannered Pekingese, always yapping. At the faintest sound, whether recognizable or not, he twitches his ears and opens his eyes. What was that? On the alert, he climbs out of his cardboard refuge to find out. If he hears the mechanical rasp of the elevator in motion, then the muffled squeaks of the elevator door opening and closing, he surmises that someone has arrived at the landing outside. Friend or enemy?

It can't be the children; they wouldn't be back from school so early. Intrigued, he listens to unfamiliar footfalls and blurred voices. Whose voices? What do they want? After some apparent hesitation on the intruders' part, the doorbell rings, not his doorbell but the one next door. Relieved, he recovers his cool and proceeds to flatten out the fur disarranged in his cardboard box. Now once again he is free to go back to sleep. But first he remembers to lap up the milk in his saucer on the windowsill in the kitchen. There he spangles the glass panes, newly washed only this morning, with fugitive hairs.

In the bedroom you can identify a cat household by the dimples that indent the eiderdown pillows moments after they have been energetically plumped back into faultless shape. In fact, every morning a tussle takes place at bedmaking time. If the mattress is temporarily exposed, the cat will clutch at one of the small, white nodes that bind it together and mold it with his sharp teeth into a ball, a mouse, or a sparrow, whatever strikes his fancy at the moment. If you try to replace the counterpane, he rolls all over it, making further difficulties.

Ah! Now he hears a loud, earsplitting buzz in the parlor nearby. Unable to determine its source, he jumps off the bed and creeps warily across the floor in the direction of the racket. As always, curiosity subdues his fear. In the parlor he vaults up to the mantel, where he can observe in safety whatever the danger is. He fixes his big, round eyes on the monstrous vacuum cleaner as if to hypnotize it, his small, round head following its every move as it advances and retreats over the carpet. But his interest flags and he turns his attention to other matters. After all, that

Susan Tantlinger: *Blue Wool*

Pierre-Pascal Furth: *On the Rue Mabillon*

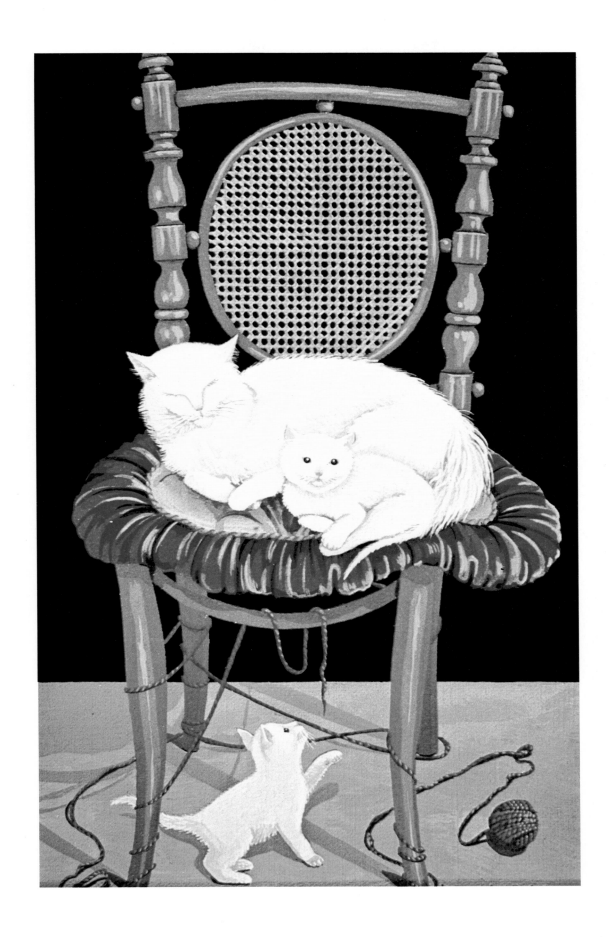

Jehanne Jouvenaud: *Playing with Yarn*

Thérèse Coustry: *The Miller's Window*

Anne Gavarni: *The Visitor*

noisy beast is only another breed of animal—and not very graceful, at that—with one advantage over him: It can purr louder.
Suddenly, it stops. Why? Perhaps it is just tired.

The excitement over, the house recovers its normal serenity,
and the cat his favorite cushion, from which nothing of such minor
moment will henceforth dislodge him. With a single exception:
the familiar click of a lamp switched on by the housemaid. The
lamp attracts him not for the unnecessary illumination it sheds
but rather for its warmth. He quits his cushion to curl up under
it.

If the lamp is turned off, he moves over to the radiator,
stretching out full length so that every part of him will receive its
benefits. With his legs dangling over the side and his chin resting
on the cast iron, once again he lapses into lethargy and dreams.

Sometimes he dreams about Rrou, the main character in a
story by Maurice Genevoix. Nowhere else, writes Genevoix,

> will a cat find so many treasures stored away behind thick
> walls as he will in a country house. Take the kitchen. There
> the cupboard doors are too slippery to scale, but there are
> always tasty morsels to find in the sink. Better yet, the solid
> rustic kitchen table is redolent with the heavenly smell of
> garlic and last night's roast lamb. On a side table stands
> Jeanne's workbasket, with a pair of shiny scissors and
> spools of thread that beckon; each spool has enough thread
> wound around it to circle the globe. But why so tightly that
> a cat can't play with it? Never mind; there are chairs and a
> stepladder to climb up and down, a doormat to sharpen
> your claws on, unless you prefer the broom, which Jeanne
> uses only to sweep the floor when the straw could serve so
> many other more entertaining purposes, and the massive
> stove, which is providentially fired every day in the cold
> weather.

The joys of a country house are infinite. The cat that knows
only urban life would love it as much as Rrou does, but with one
reservation: a radiator warms you all over, whereas a stove gets so
hot that you approach it at your own peril.

But the kitchen table with its tempting odors is a sheer delight.
The city table with nothing better than a Formica top is a bore. It
never smells of anything, and it's cold on the paws after you've
spent so much time warming them.

All these thoughts dry the cat's throat. He opens his mouth

Agnès Emanuelli: *The Naughty Cat Hides*

Odile Gaillard: *Beflowered*

Mimi Vang Olsen: *Three Calico Friends*

Mimi Vang Olsen: *Cat in a Crock*

and tongues his arid palate, stretches out both ends, yawns to relax his jaws, licks himself briefly, then stops to think: which will it be, the water in the bowl of lilies, easily accessible, or the water from the tap? He can open the tap with one stroke of a paw and let the water gush out—more refreshing than the stale liquid left for him every morning on the floor, good enough for the dog but not for him. He chooses the tap. With a bound, he lands on the drainboard, sits, and lets the water flow; head back, his nose under the tap, he drinks with rapid flicks of the tongue. With one paw he dries the stray drops that bead his moustache by smoothing them out on his cheeks. His thirst slaked, muscles relaxed, and body still warm from his last siesta, he decides to do setting-up exercises, to make sure he keeps himself in top form.

The best exercise of all is, of course, to chase your tail and hold it down if you can. Rushing madly around and around is especially good for the circulation. But not for the room. The decor will be somewhat modified: the rattan chair meant to stand beside the round oak table will be leaning crazily against it; the curtain ropes and crimson tassels will have performed fanciful arabesques; and more.

Thus, those who live in a cat household are not likely to become bored with the unrelieved monotony of their interior arrangements, which undergo a constant process of renovation. Every day brings its surprises, promising never-ending change and suggesting that it is never advisable to take anything for granted.

Once the kitten has recovered from the wrench he suffered when his new master separated him from the place of his birth—and his mother's sublime reed basket, which he will never forget—he resents any further displacements; he has spent too much time and energy adapting himself to his new quarters, ferreting out its secrets, investigating what lies beyond the cracks under the doors, figuring out the function of the doorknobs, and so forth. To go off on a solitary excursion is stimulating, but to be squeezed at vacation time into the backseat of a car among valises, parcels, and squirming children during the long journey to the seaside is another. Obliged to leave the home he has made his own and accommodate himself to some strange environment for one interminable month, only to be hauled back again, is too much to ask of him.

Brought home before he has had enough time to acclimatize

Christine Cipriano: *Siamese with Blue Flowers*
Bernard Prillieux: *Lady of the Manor*

Anne Gavarni: *On the Riviera*

Anne-Marie Sabatier: *Barging on the Seine*

Saint-Côme: *The Scholar*

Fanny Darnat: *Riton*

himself to the salty air, to say nothing of the vast, alarming expanse of space and sea, he always arrives with shattered nerves. Fortunately, however, his adopted family has finally come to understand what has caused his holiday blues and has agreed to leave him every summer in his beloved home. He requires unbroken regularity; indeed, he wants everyone to come and go on fixed schedules, not to keep odd hours.

Like the pet cat of Joris-Karl Huysmans, who was

affectionate and sly, but slightly unbalanced. She could never countenance a whim or any departure from normal routine. She expected you to go to bed and get up at exactly the same time. Whenever she was discontented about anything, her master could instantly detect the resentment in her eyes. Whenever he came home before eleven o'clock in the evening, she would be waiting for him, clawing at the front door and meowing vigorously even before he set foot in the vestibule.

Then she would roll her languorous gold-green eyes, rub against his trousered leg, jump on the furniture, rise up on her hind legs like a rearing colt, and relish his loving pats on her head. But if he returned after eleven, she refused to greet him; she would only rise to her feet when he stroked her and arch her back, rejecting his caresses. She would not budge and snarled if he patted her on the head or scratched under her chin.

Certainly, it is most irksome to wait up for a beloved one who stays out until all hours. A cat will calm his anxiety in sleep, but then the latecomer wakens him, abruptly and without warning, from some enchanting reverie. To convey his displeasure, he will refuse to welcome you with open paws or an affectionate purr, but neither will he claw your hand if you reach out to him.

Yet cats have many admirable traits, among them an appreciation for music and other suggestive sounds. Surrounded by the family as he listens to Beethoven on the radio, he seems to swell up with the same sense of well-being he derives from the warm radiator or the lamp's halo. If the record player suddenly jolts him out of a nap, he will get to his feet, stretch his neck, and spread himself out as he listens with obvious pleasure. Marcel Jouhandeau's music-loving puss will press his snout against the loudspeaker and sometimes try to snatch the notes out of the air.

Cellia Saubry: *The Puss-in-Boots Shop*

Monique Valdeneige: *The Lovers of Rhama*

Susan Tantlinger: *The Music Lover*

Pierre-Pascal Furth: *Nestor and Lampion*

Madeleine Marcoux: *Sharing the Warmth*

Susan Tantlinger: *On an Oriental Rug*

When the music stops, he examines the record player to find out why and waits for the music to begin again.

Apart from music, other sounds beguile his ear, most of all his master's well-modulated, soothing voice; shouts and strident tones will send him flying. He also likes to hear cracker crumbs scratching against his cardboard box when the housemaid shakes it out, the can opener on the tin or milk plashing into his saucer with an appeal not altogether aesthetic, and the squeak of the mattress when his master slips under the bedcovers to sink into his long night's rest.

The pampered cat will take this as an invitation to join him, and curl up at the foot of the bed. The man is therefore obliged to sleep only in positions that will not disturb him; his cat will not tolerate kicks or exasperating shifts from one side to the other. In this contest of wills, the softhearted master never wins.

Take the baker's cat. No one has ever been able to shoo him off the top of the glass counter once he has decided to install himself there, whether or not the place is jammed with customers. Sometimes he will go to supervise the work in the back room where the bread is being baked, or lie flat on the cashier's desk, head back to keep watch on the entry door. Wherever he is, he makes himself altogether at home.

In his New York apartment, Jean-Claude Suares, writer, art director, and filmmaker, once clocked the activities of his cat minute by minute and recorded the results in his book *The Indispensable Cat:*

> During the last twenty-four hours, he has spent seven hours and twenty minutes sleeping on my bed, and five hours sleeping on the sofa. He gazed out of the window for twenty-five minutes and lay in the sun at the kitchen window for an hour and a half. He spent ten minutes chasing a fly (but failed to catch it) and eight minutes playing with my twenty-five dollar silver shaving brush, which has vanished, probably forever. He spent the remaining time inspecting the apartment, crawling in and out of closets, clambering up on chairs and shelves, without once knocking over a vase or a plant. His one meal of the day, at 9:15 in the morning, took him six minutes to eat, after which he licked himself all over, a daily routine that requires about sixteen minutes of his time—five for the paws, four for the breast, four and a half for the shoulders and the rest to wash

Christian Sylvain: *The Sun-Room*

Simone Castex: *Romeo*

Monique Valdeneige: *Visiting My Aunt and Her Cats*

his tail and ears. (He dampens his paws to clean his ears.) This is the apartment cat's typical day, evolved over centuries of cohabiting with man. Unlike restless human beings, he is satisfied with the circumscribed space allotted him, therefore appears in some ways better suited to city life than his master.

With all these data at hand, who can say that a household deprived of a cat is as cheerful as one with a cat?

Conditioned by millennia of well-being, always appearing to take only the good things life has to offer, "the cat we live with is the warm, furry, moustached, purring memory of a lost paradise," says Léonor Fini. With his special past, his unassailable mystery and magic, he will render his immediate surroundings, whether a living room, an attic, a bakery, a hayloft, or an oil-spattered harbor barge, a more lived-in and a friendlier place than any other.

Biographies of
the Artists

Evelyne Blot
Born in Paris and brought up in Sèvres, Evelyne Blot began her career in the early 1970s in television and created a popular video series of animated cartoons titled "Les Glops." Since 1975 she has been traveling constantly by ship, sending her canvases from every part of the globe to the Galerie Naïfs et Primitifs in Paris. Her special subjects are animals and nature, particularly the sea.

Simone Castex
Born in 1907 at St. Hilaire-des-Loges in the Vendée, Simone Castex wavered for a long time between the medical profession and painting and settled the matter by attending the Arts Décoratifs at the age of twenty. After exhibiting at the Bois and Bobler galleries in Paris, she founded a studio of design at the Institut Bellan. Since 1979 she has been showing scenes from her childhood at the Galerie Naïfs et Primitifs. In 1983 she collaborated as illustrator on a picture book titled *Paris et les naïfs.*

Christine Cipriano
Although a graduate in art history, during a period of unemployment Christine Cipriano, a native Parisian, took up painting; among her early efforts, she illustrated Hans Christian Andersen's story "The Snow Queen." In 1979 and 1983 she exhibited at the Galerie Naïfs et Primitifs in Paris and New York, in 1984 at the Salon of Naïf Art in Paris, and in the same year in Geneva, Switzerland. Her art extols eternal childhood in scenes of silent gardens and broad meadows.

Thérèse Coustry
Belgian by birth, Thérèse Coustry set up her easel in 1975 and four years later began exhibiting in Belgium, The Netherlands, and at the Galerie Naïfs et Primitifs in Paris and New York. In 1979 she won the first prize awarded a Belgian artist for outstanding merit. She has collaborated on two illustrated volumes, *Les naïfs belges* and *Le paradis et les naïfs.* Her canvases depict a charming peasant world with a nostalgia for the past.

Fanny Darnat
After studying at the Arts et Métiers, Fanny Darnat became a fashion designer but later joined the roster of artists allied with the Galerie Naïfs et Primitifs. In 1978 she exhibited in Washington, D.C., and the following year at the Art Expo in Basel, Switzerland. In October 1984 she had a one-woman show in New York. Precise and punctilious, her art is imbued with a singularly nostalgic and poetic superrealism.

Patricia de Breuvery
Daughter of the designer Hervé, Patricia de Breuvery was already designing textiles at an early age but in 1980 decided to devote her talents entirely to painting, showing her work at the Galerie Naïfs et Primitifs in Paris and New York. Two years later, she contributed illustrations to *Paris et les Naïfs.* Given to realism, she nevertheless brings the freshness of naïve art to her landscapes of Brittany and Provence.

Demonchy
In 1918, at the age of 4, Demonchy was orphaned. At 13 he was hired as a farm boy, "receiving a good many kicks in the rear for marking up the stable walls with crayon drawings." Later he obtained a job with the French State Railways; nonetheless, he always found time to gratify his love of painting. Encouraged by a friend and admirer, he has exhibited all over the world. Among his collectors he counts André Breton and Max-Pol Fouchet, while Anatole Jakovsky has published a monograph on his work. Now retired, he continues to paint.

Maria de Posz
An artist of international fame, Hungarian by birth, Maria de Posz has lived in Venezuela and Salzburg, Austria. Since 1966 her works have been seen in Salzburg, Vienna, Caracas, Zurich, Basel, and Lugano. Her canvases combine realism with the naïve style and reveal an immense warmth and love for her subjects. She has collaborated on numerous illustrated books.

Agnès Emanuelli
An inveterate traveler, Agnès Emanuelli launched her career as an interpreter in Singapore and Caracas and later lived for a time in Louisiana. Returning to her native France, she painted her impressions of the world she knows on brightly colored canvases. She now divides her time between Paris and her country home, and her work between television and painting, which she exhibits at the Galerie Naïfs et Primitifs in Paris and New York. In 1983 she contributed illustrations to *Paris et les naïfs*.

Andréa Emery
Andréa Emery studied for two years at the Beaux-Arts in Paris, mastering an ancient technique in oil painting. She has exhibited in Provence in 1979 and at the Galerie Naïfs et Primitifs in Paris since 1982. Her canvases are distinctive for their soft, warm, romantic colors. For the publishing house Garnier, she illustrated *Enfer d'enfer*, and for Magnard a volume on ecology, *Le sang est salé comme l'océan*, issued in 1984.

André-Yves Fey
Born in Paris in 1938, André-Yves Fey attended the Beaux-Arts in Hastings, subsequently worked as assistant film director with Cocteau, Christian-Jacque, Preminger, and Schoendorfer. Now a television director, he spends his free time painting seascapes illuminated by the light of the midnight sun. To turn out a good painting, he says, "you must first of all catch the most significant moment of a story as it unfolds in your imagination."

Pierre-Pascal Furth
Born in Mulhouse in 1948 in the family quarters over a modest shop run by his parents, Pierre-Pascal Furth studied letters in his home town but completed his formal education in Paris. He has been variously employed as a secondary school instructor, plumber, magazine writer, and journalist for *Revue Europe* and *Le Monde*, meanwhile spending his evenings painting small, realistic scenes in minute detail that reveal his admiration for the Flemish masters and nineteenth-century landscape artists.

Odile Gaillard
After studying at the Beaux-Arts in Angers, Odile Gaillard, a native of Les Deux Sèvres, went on to design fabrics and carve toys out of wood. In 1973 she cofounded a regional theater that made its debut at the Avignon Festival; in 1977 she abandoned these pursuits to paint. She has shown her works in Agde, Nancy, Rennes, St. Brieuc, and, since 1979, at the Galerie Naïfs et Primitifs. Among her accomplishments, she has illustrated a book on the subject of her childhood home.

Marta Gaspar
Born in Argentina in 1961, Marta Gaspar has exhibited in Rosario, Santa Fe, Cordoba, and at the Museum of Modern Art in Buenos Aires. Now a French resident, she exhibits at the Galerie Naïfs et Primitifs. In 1983 she took part in the Bestiaire Naïfs exhibition at Levallois-Perret. Her brightly colored canvases depict the lush vegetation of the jungles in her native land.

Anne Gavarni
Granddaughter of a Second Empire lithographer and daughter of a painter, Anne Gavarni hails from Bois-Colombes. Her first efforts, engravings and etchings, were introduced to the public by Gisèle d'Assailly. Taking up the palette, she now paints imaginary landscapes, fabulous animals, delicate bouquets of flowers, and little people bursting with vitality. Her works were displayed in various salons before she joined the Galerie Naïfs et Primitifs.

Agnès Godard
Born in Paris in 1952, Agnès Godard lived in her childhood with her family in a big house surrounded by a spacious garden, which still wields a persuasive influence over her. Beginning with quilt- and lace-making, eventually she turned to painting secret houses, beaches dotted with parasols, and portraits of children playing on the seashore.

Jehanne Jouvenaud
At first, Jehanne Jouvenaud lent her talents to industrial design, painting on silk, and decorating building façades; weary of urban life, however, she retired to the country and dedicated herself to art. She now exhibits at the Galerie Naïfs et Primitifs in Paris, and New York. Paradoxically, the very city she fled—Paris, with its parks, streets, and kiosks—provides the theme of her art.

Arlette Laville
Because Arlette Laville, born in Lons-le-Saunier in 1938, is a teacher by profession, she cannot spend as much time at her easel as she would like; all the same, in her spare time she manages to paint pictures of houses, parks, domestic animals, and children in the primitivist manner.

Brigitte Mailliet

Brought up in Versailles, Brigitte Mailliet learned to draw under the tutelage of René Aubert. Her schooling finished, she studied stage design at the Arts Décoratifs but gave up her theatrical aspirations to teach, and at the same time painting, for the most part, cats, free in nature. She has been a client of the Galerie Naïfs et Primitifs since 1981; in 1983 she exhibited at the Bestiaire Naïf.

Madeleine Marcoux

Born in 1924 in Blois, Madeleine Marcoux earned her way as a corporate secretary until 1977, when she decided to become an artist. Her subjects include smiling children, happy cats, radiant gardens in small format, and the sea, which she paints in broad brushstrokes. In 1979 she exhibited at the Espace Marengo in Angoulême, and in 1982 and 1983 at the Galerie Naïfs et Primitifs. The artist professes a special admiration for the Flemish masters, Italian primitivists, and the Impressionists.

Valentin Marcq

Valentin Marcq was born in Paris in 1921. In his youth he studied art at the Testard Academy by day and the nude at the Grande Chaumière at night. Thereafter a journalist, he wrote for *France-Soir* and *Le Monde* until 1965, when he began to paint seriously. Discovered by the Galerie Naïfs et Primitifs, his work was first exhibited at the Basel Fair in 1977 and again in 1978, in 1979 at the Washington Fair, and in 1980 at the Forum des Halles.

Bernard Partiot

Bernard Partiot won an enviable reputation for his creative ideas as an art director but gave up that profession to dedicate himself exclusively to painting scenes from nature, with which he feels a close affinity, especially the reflection of light on water. He has exhibited his works at the Salon des Indépendants, in various Parisian galleries and, between 1977 and 1983, in Basel, Chicago, New York, and at the International Salon of Naïf Art in 1984. In Paris he is now represented by the Galerie Naïfs et Primitifs.

Gisèle Pierlot

In her childhood, Gisèle Pierlot already displayed an exceptional talent for drawing, but her family, although devotees of the arts, never took her passion seriously. She therefore put her brushes aside for a number of years until she found the courage to take them up again. Her excellent views of ancient shops in Paris and the provinces were first unveiled in 1977 at the Galerie Naïfs et Primitifs. She has also contributed illustrations to *Paris et les naïfs*.

Bernard Prillieux

Claiming Munich, Germany, as his birthplace, Bernard Prillieux studied humanities before becoming a world traveler, all the time painting constantly. He sometimes takes as long as two or three years to complete a work to his satisfaction and prefers small formats, which are perfectly suited to the minutiae of his style. The Galerie Naïfs et Primitifs introduced his marvelous world to the public in 1980.

Annie Rétivat

A fashion designer before she became an artist, Annie Rétivat entrusted her first paintings to a Swiss art gallery, which has been selling them ever since. The Galerie Naïfs et Primitifs mounted her first one-woman show in 1978 and repeated it in 1980 and 1982. In 1983 she exhibited in Chicago and contributed illustrations to *Paris et les naïfs*. In their elusive atmosphere, her scenes are tinged with nostalgia.

Didier Richard

Didier Richard was born in Rennes into an intellectual world with a strong appreciation of the arts. After winning honors for his achievements as a university student, he elected to follow a dual career as teacher and painter. A passionate colorist, he constantly searches for new effects with a limited palette. He had his first show at the Galerie Naïfs et Primitifs in 1983 and in the same year contributed illustrations to *Paris et les naïfs*.

Anne-Marie Sabatier

A Parisian by birth and preference, Anne-Marie Sabatier initiated her art career painting in the streets of Montmartre, also on occasion in Saint-Tropez, and contributing to newspapers as an illustrator. She made her debut as an artist at the Antoinette Gallery in Paris in 1975 and showed at the 1977 Beaux-Arts International in the Grand Palais, and also four times at the Salon d'Automne between 1977 and 1981. Her illustrations are included in *Paris et les naïfs*.

Saint-Côme

Saint-Côme emigrated to France from Barcelona and spent his youth in Paris during the turbulent 1930s. He was a friend of such notables as Cocteau, Bérard, Marlene Dietrich, and Marie-Laure de Noailles. In 1940 his *trompe-l'oeil* illustrations began to appear in the American edition of *Vogue*. In 1950 he struck out for Oceania, where he spent fifteen years as chef and crocodile hunter, but always with his paint box at hand. In 1964 he returned to France, settled in Marseilles and wrote a book about his exotic adventures in the South Pacific. He is represented by the Galerie Naïfs et Primitifs.

Cellia Saubry

During business hours, Cellia Saubry, of Rouen, worked as a medical secretary; in the evening, however, she re-created on canvas the monuments of Paris, the English countryside, and houses in suburbia. Under the aegis of a Parisian art dealer, she won notable successes in Paris, Switzerland, and New York. In 1980 she joined forces with the Galerie Naïfs et Primitifs in Paris and New York and designed illustrations for *Paris et les naïfs*. Her work was also shown at the 1983 Salon International d'Art Naïf.

Magdalena Shummer

Of Polish origin, Magdalena Shummer set up her easel in 1961 and began to paint. She traveled widely in Europe but eventually emigrated to the United States. Her portraits, landscapes, and still lifes are distinctive for their poetic realism. In 1977 she exhibited at the Wessel Library, in 1979 at the Morris Gallery, and in 1981 at the Studio Gallery. Her art is now a permanent feature at the Galerie Naïfs et Primitifs.

Sophie Sirot
Still in her young womanhood, Paris-born Sophie Sirot followed the man in her life to Africa, where she was entranced by the blazing colors of the luxuriant tropical forest and the translucent light. Returning to France in 1972, she made her home in Brittany to take her degree in the plastic arts and the history of art. Her canvases, pictorial memoirs of her travels, have been on exhibition at the Galerie Naïfs et Primitifs since 1977. Her illustrations are also to be seen in *Paris et les naïfs*.

Christian Sylvain
A Breton by birth, Christian Sylvain studied literature and taught French in Morocco before discovering the joy of painting. In 1977 he opened an antiques shop in Montpellier; in 1982 he accepted an offer to manage a fruit orchard near Avignon. In 1983 he showed his work for the first time at the Galerie Naïfs et Primitifs, which followed his debut with several other shows during that same eventful year.

Françoise Syx
Bored with her job as an industrial designer, Françoise Syx abandoned it to paint, adopting an old "tempera-and-oil" technique ideally suited to her portrayals of animals, gardens peopled by children, and radiant nature. Her first shows led to the inaugural exhibition at the Museum of Art in Nice. In 1983 she joined the Galerie Naïfs et Primitifs, where her paintings are permanently on show.

Zofia Szalowska
Zofia Szalowska left Poland to study at the Beaux-Arts in Paris and subsequently became a French resident. Specializing in portraiture, a medium in which she excels, she first exhibited in Cologne in 1975 and, a year later, began showing regularly at the Galerie Naïfs et Primitifs, both in Paris and New York. Her work has also been seen in Basel, at the 1979 Art Expo in Washington, and in the "Genius of the Naïfs" exposition at the Grand Palais in Paris.

Susan Tantlinger
An American born in 1950, Susan Tantlinger ran a studio for painting on fabrics until she opened her own shop in San Francisco. After moving to France, she now follows a dual career as a fashion designer and an artist. Her canvases were seen at the Bestiaire Naïf exposition in Levallois-Perret in 1983 and at the 1984 International Salon of Naïf Art. In the latter year she exhibited a series of amusing works at the Galerie Naïfs et Primitifs.

Setsuko Uno
Born in Tokyo in 1954, Setsuko Uno spent her university years studying traditional Japanese painting, sculpture, and design and became a doll-maker under the tutelage of Tomonaga Akamitsu. Transferring to France, she studied Western art at the Beaux-Arts in Tours. After showings in various galleries, she joined the roster of artists represented by the Galerie Naïfs et Primitifs in 1979. Her precise, delicate lines and subdued colors are reminiscent of Japanese art.

Monique Valdeneige

Monique Valdeneige took her training at the Arts Appliqués in Paris, then joined the public relations organization Publicis as layout assistant, eventually advancing to the rank of artistic director; but success failed to overcome the irresistible appeal that drew her to painting. She had her first show at the Galerie Naïfs et Primitifs in 1978, another in 1980, and a third in 1982. She also exhibits in Grenoble and in New York. She is a profound admirer of Monet.

Mimi Vang Olsen

A child of the Bronx, New York, Mimi Vang Olsen has two passions, painting and animals, which she combines by putting one at the service of the other. She portrays cats, her favorite of all animals, on large canvases, either in individual poses or in the company of their adopted families. After living for twelve years in Denmark, she has returned to the United States, where she exhibits frequently.

Marie-Hélène Véran

When Marie-Hélène Véran took the competitive entrance examinations at the Arts Décoratifs in Cannes, the director of the institute found her talent already so well developed that he dissuaded her from taking classes. Showing first at the Odile Varel Gallery in Vence, in 1979 she became an artist-member of the Galerie Naïfs et Primitifs and now exhibits in Paris and New York. Her night scenes and lush, quiet views of her native Provence are infused with admirable sensitivity.